TABLE OF CONTENTS

CHAPTER I

INTRODUCTION

The Intermediate-range Nuclear Forces (INF) Treaty, which was signed by the United States and the Soviet Union on 8 December 1987, created differences among NATO allies over NATO's military strategy, the modernization of the western nuclear arsenals, and future arms control negotiations.

NATO's current military strategy--Flexible Response--has been successful in meeting its objective since it was established in 1967. Flexible Response is based upon a flexible and balanced range of appropriate responses, conventional and nuclear, to all levels of aggression or threat of aggression. This strategy has rested upon strategic nuclear, theater nuclear, and conventional forces; the so-called NATO TRIAD.

The INF Treaty eliminates a specific category (500-5,500 kilometers range) of American and Soviet ground based nuclear missiles from Europe. NATO European allies fear that NATO will lose an essential part of their strike capacity against Soviet territory and will lose a reliable and decisive part of their escalation options. By eliminating the theater nuclear deterrent, the treaty will lead to NATO's increasing reliance on conventional forms of deterrence which the member nations do not feel are credible against the Warsaw Pact.

They also fear that the removal of US
intermediate-range nuclear missiles from their territory
represents only the first phase of a large reduction in
America's defense commitment to Europe. They believe that the
US ground-based missiles in Europe were necessary to guarantee
that the US nuclear forces would be engaged in the event of a
nuclear war in Europe. This was referred to as "coupling" or
"linkage." The INF Treaty will serve to decouple the US
strategic deterrent from Europe's defense by eliminating
equitable nuclear risk-sharing among alliance members.

NATO is even more deeply divided over the question of
whether to include short-range nuclear weapons in the
conventional stability talks. The Soviet Union has long
advocated including short-range and tactical nuclear weapons in
conventional arms talks as a follow-on to the "zero-zero" option
to eliminate both superpowers' intermediate-range nuclear arms
from Europe. West Germany also supports adopting the "third
zero" which would also do away with tactical nuclear weapons
because German territory is located fully within the reach of
the remaining short-range missiles, while a considerably reduced
risk exists for some other allies. Germany believes that the
INF Treaty leads to creation of zones of differing security. On
the other hand, Britain and France worry that removal of
tactical weapons would make western Europe even more vulnerable
to a conventional attack from the east. The two European
nuclear powers are eager to retain their independent nuclear

arsenals and thus are reluctant to include their tactical nuclear weapons in any conventional arms talks with the Soviets.

Turkey shares a 610 kilometers long common border with the USSR and is especially concerned about the INF Treaty's effects on its security.

CHAPTER II

BACKGROUND

Intermediate-range Nuclear Missiles

Soviet Union has deployed intermediate-range missiles since the late 1950s. These systems could threaten most or all of NATO Europe, but not reach the United States. The United States deployed no such missiles in Europe after the mid-1960s. In arms control terms, these systems were not considered "strategic." They were therefore excluded from the arms control limits in the SALT process.

In 1977, the Soviet Union began to deploy the SS-20. It was a substantial improvement over its predecessors. It had longer range, greater accuracy, and enhanced mobility. Moreover, it had three independently targetable warheads, whereas the previous systems had only one. NATO political leaders and military authorities carefully assessed this new threat and consulted extensively on how to counter it. They were concerned that, if left unmatched, this new capability could lead Moscow into believing that it could intimidate the alliance or even cause the Soviet Union to miscalculate the risks of aggression. To prevent this, the NATO foreign and defense ministers adopted what has come to be called the "dual-track" decision in 1979.

On one track, the United States would begin to deploy 572 single-warhead intermediate-range missiles in the United

Kingdom (UK), Italy, Belgium, the Federal Republic of Germany (FRG), and the Netherlands in 1983. At the same time, on a second track, the United States would attempt to negotiate limits on US and Soviet INF missiles at the lowest possible level. The INF Treaty was signed almost eight years to the day after the 1979 dual-track decision was taken.[1:5-8]

The INF Treaty and Its Importance

The INF Treaty President Reagan and Soviet leader Gorbachev signed in Washington on 8 December 1987 calls for the elimination of all US and Soviet land-based nuclear missiles with ranges of between 300 and 3,400 miles (500-5,500 kilometers) over a 3-year period. The impact of the treaty on the nuclear force structures of the USA and the USSR will be significant:

-- The USA will destroy 120 deployed Pershing II missiles and 309 deployed ground-launched cruise missiles.

-- The USSR will destroy 405 deployed SS-20 Saber missiles, 65 deployed SS-4 Sandal missiles, 220 deployed shorter-range (300-600 miles) SS-12 Scaleboard missiles, and 167 deployed SS-23 Spider missiles.

-- Approximately 520 US and 2,150 Soviet nuclear warheads will be deactivated.[2:4]

The treaty calls for the most intrusive verification measures ever included in a nuclear arms agreement. US inspectors will be based at a Soviet missile production facility in Votkins for 13 years, while Soviet inspectors will be based at a facility in Utah for the same period. Representatives of

5

both sides also will be allowed to inspect missile production factories on short notice.[3:678]

The INF Treaty's true value lies in controlling the arms race. It is the first international treaty that will result in a destruction of recently deployed, first-line nuclear weapons. The older SALT I and II Treaties established ceilings, but did not serve to reduce total numbers or capability. They did require the dismantling of some weapons systems, but only older ones already scheduled to be retired and abolished. The ABM Treaty went further in banning deployment of a new type of weapon system, but it brought about no real disarmament.

The greatest political benefit of the INF Treaty is the new types of verification it provides. The verification process represents a dramatic increase in recognition by the both sides of the principle of common security: shared limits on arms and shared information about arms increase security on both sides.

The treaty is also important for Europeans. From the European perspective, the greater the level of tension between the superpowers, the greater the prospect of military confrontation. Conversely, the fear of confrontation recedes when the United States and the Soviet Union are engaged in talks to lessen tensions, especially on the reduction of arms.

The treaty has only limited value as a means of reversing the arms race--unless it is a door to something more. It eliminates less than five percent of all nuclear weapons and will not have much impact on the destructiveness of a nuclear war.

6

CHAPTER III

MILITARY CONSEQUENCES OF THE TREATY

NATO Cohesion Must Continue

Although I don't plan to examine all the political consequences of the treaty, I will mention one of them that I think is very important. The INF Treaty creates differences amongst the allies over NATO's future. This affects NATO cohesion negatively. NATO cohesion, as well as NATO capability, plays a vital role in NATO deterrence. Deterrence requires both capability and will, and mutual cohesion ensures adequate will to use the capability.

The reasons for forming the NATO alliance originally remain valid concerns for the allies today. The North Atlantic Treaty, one of the western countermeasures in the Cold War against the threat of aggression by the Soviet Union, was aimed at safeguarding the freedom of the Atlantic community. By considering an armed attack on any member as an attack against them all, the treaty provided for collective self-defense. The principal objective of the arrangement was to neutralize Soviet power in eastern Europe by formally linking American nuclear power to the protection of western Europe.

But now, Mr Gorbachev is trying to convince the NATO allies that the USSR is no longer a threat to them. Soviet foreign policy has changed since Mr Gorbachev became General

Secretary of the Communist Party. He frequently argues that Soviet preoccupation with the modernization of its economy and society assures the peaceful nature of the USSR's global strategy. This is probably true to the extent that a period of international calm would help the Kremlin devote more resources to economic development. This does not mean that Mr Gorbachev departs from the fundamentals of Soviet strategy. On the contrary, in this period the Soviet Union will be able to concentrate its efforts to drive the allies apart politically. Because Moscow's peace image has been magnified in United States and European thinking, it is more likely to succeed in this long-term effort.

However, Mr Gorbachev could fall from power. Economic failure or internal power struggles could force him to return to hostility toward the west. For these reasons, strong NATO cohesiveness is more important now than it ever was before.

Flexible Response and Extended Deterrence

The INF Treaty has intensified discussions about NATO's flexible response strategy, the future of extended deterrence, and the modernization of nuclear forces assigned to the European theater. It also has focused increased attention on NATO's conventional force posture, its modernization, and conventional arms control.

The doctrine of flexible response became the basis of NATO's military strategy in 1967 in order to provide a more credible replacement for the earlier doctrine of "massive

retaliation" because of strategic parity between the
superpowers. It was aimed at ensuring the credibility of the US
nuclear guarantee to Europe without sacrificing the flexibility
to respond to a Soviet attack with a range of military options
from conventional to strategic weapons. "It means that the
alliance must have sufficient forces to respond to any level of
aggression and must possess a full spectrum of forces so that it
can counter any act of aggression with an appropriate response.
NATO forces are made up of three interlocking elements known as
the NATO TRIAD. They are: (1) conventional forces strong
enough to resist and repel a conventional attack on a limited
scale, and to sustain a conventional defense in the forward
areas against large-scale conventional aggression; (2)
intermediate and short-range nuclear forces to enhance the
deterrent and if necessary, the defensive effort of NATO's
conventional forces against a conventional attack; to deter and
defend against an attack with nuclear forces of the same kind;
and to provide a linkage to the strategic nuclear forces of the
alliance with the aim of convincing an aggressor that any form
of attack on NATO could result in very serious damage to his
interests and emphasizing the dangers implicit in continuing a
conflict; and (3) US and UK strategic nuclear forces which
provide the ultimate deterrent."[4:27]

By eliminating those theater nuclear weapons having the
most deterrent value--the capability to threaten Moscow in 15

9

minutes from European soil--the INF Treaty causes the NATO's strategy of flexible response to lose credibility. This credibility needs to be restored, but the alliance is deeply divided over how to restore it.

The French and British believe it is important to modernize the residual force of short-range nuclear weapons. Fear of a denuclearized Europe motivates the French and British desire to modernize short-range nuclear weapons (SNF), which have been excluded from the list of arms control priorities set by NATO's Nuclear Planning Group.[5:35] They maintain that the elimination of ground launched cruise missiles and Pershing II missiles will weaken flexible responses by depriving NATO of intermediate-range options on the escalation ladder. Modernization of the Lance missile and the deployment of a standoff missile on the NATO aircraft, in their view, are the optimal solutions to the problem. In short, the British Government remains strongly committed to the implementation of the 1983 Montebello decision. This decision, taken during a meeting of NATO ministers at Motebello, Canada, committed the alliance to yet another "two-track" approach to arms control and modernization. The arms control track (already completed) mandated a reduction of 1,400 shorter-range nuclear weapons from the American nuclear stocks in Europe. The modernization track promised initiatives to replace or upgrade the remaining weapons, including a new generation missile to replacce the Lance, a new "stand-off" weapon and a thorough modernization of

NATO's nuclear capable artilery.[6:130] Both France and the United States also strongly support this course of action.

However, West Germany and some of the smaller NATO members, including Norway, Denmark, and the Netherlands are strongly opposed to the implementation of the Montebello decision. The Soviet Union has long advocated including short-range and tactical nuclear weapons in conventional arms talks as a follow-on to the "zero-zero" option to eliminate both superpowers intermediate-range nuclear arms from Europe. West Germany particularly supports adopting the "third zero": to do away with tactical nuclear weapons completely. West Germany is certain to resist the deployment of new short-range nuclear weapons for fear of having more inviting targets for Soviet weapons on their soil. They contend that SNF should have been removed first because these weapons are deployed on the forward edge of the battle area and can be overrun by advancing forces. This would make their existence and use problematic--to use or lose them.

Many German defense analysts reject the notion that the INF Treaty has impaired extended deterrence, a view shared by Americans who favor arms control. They argue that NATO will still possess enough nuclear weapons after the removal of INF with which to target the Soviet Union, e.g., short-range ballistic missiles, artillery shells, and dual capable aircraft capable of delivering tactical nuclear weapons. Furthermore, NATO will retain the 400 Poseidon submarine-launched ballistic

11

missiles assigned to the SACCEUR and nuclear-armed sea-launched cruise missiles (SLCMs) on US warships patrolling NATO waters.[5:36] In addition, the French as well as the British nuclear deterrents are available in the event of a crisis.

These differences among the allies has created the uncertainty that the alliance would implement the Montebello decision. It promised initiatives to replace or upgrade the remaining weapons, including a new generation missile to replace the Lance, a new standoff weapon and thorough modernization of NATO's nuclear-capable artillery. None of the critical modernization has been undertaken.

What should the solution be? Both sides are partially correct in their arguments. By 1992, when the INF missiles have been withdrawn, about 3,250 US nuclear warheads will remain on European soil.[2:4] The vast majority of these warheads are battlefield weapons that could be overrun before there would be sufficient time for political consultation among the allies for their release. In terms of the crisis stability, these weapons have a potential problem, if deterrence fails. Moreover, none of them is capable of striking Soviet territory. Given the alliances' defensive strategy, nearly all of these weapons would be firing at targets on NATO soil.

The range of nuclear artillery is known (about 20 miles). The Soviets maximum-range ground-to-ground missile is the SS-1 (SCUD-B) which can reach targets up to 300 kilometers away. Most analysts, however, consider the SS-1 too inaccurate for attacks against most military targets, except perhaps in a chemical mode. That leaves only the highly accurate 120 kilometers range SS-21 for operations against runways, command and control centers, and equipment storage areas. The INF Treaty cuts down the tactical depth of both NATO and Warsaw Pact missile forces. Both sides will undoubtedly upgrade their tactical missile forces with increased ranges approaching the 500 kilometers as allowed by the treaty. The United States is already developing an improved Lance missile with a range of nearly 250 kilometers, well beyond the 70 kilometers range of today's Lance. Obviously, similar improvements of the SS-21 and SCUD missiles are also underway on the Soviet side.

Those increased ranges would help increase the allies' consultation time, but would expose more West German (and some other NATO countries' territories) to the reach of these new short-range missiles. These countries will now need some sort of anti-missile system. It could be argued that by reducing the overall missile threat, the INF Treaty has killed interest in anti-tactical missile systems. Regardless of the INF Treaty, NATO's air defense systems will require modernization. These systems must be dual capable, anti-air/anti-missile for the reasons already given.

Submarine-launched ballistic missiles (SLBMs), while certainly capable of striking targets on Soviet territory, are not configured for the more discriminate missions assigned to theater weapons. Furthermore, to avoid early escalation to the

13

strategic level, NATO--especially the United States--also would be reluctant to use these SLBM warheads. Submarine-launched cruise missiles (SLCMs) are operationally suitable, but the ships on which they are deployed have multiple missions and are not assigned permanently to the European theater. One possible solution would be to maintain a minimum number of SLCMs chopped to SACEUR on various platforms much the same way SLBMs are chopped to SACEUR now.

British and French Governments have repeatedly declared that their nuclear forces (which will grow significantly over the next decade*) are national deterrents to be used only in the event of national catastrophe. Such declarations are politically understandable but strategically wrong. If they want to avoid denuclearization, they should link their nuclear arsenals to NATO theater nuclear forces in some way. Otherwise, what the Germans proclaim would be accepted as a true. It is by eliminating equitable nuclear risk-sharing that the INF Treaty creates different security zones.

---

*France is planning to deploy its "Hades" missiles in 1991, which will have a range of 450 kilometers (replacing the 120-kilometer Pluton) and develop the longer-range S-4 missile. In addition, French Mirage IV-2000 and Super Etendards are being equipped with new medium-range air-to-ground missile which has a range of 200-300 kilometers.(5:36) The Thatcher government determined to modernize Britain's nuclear deterrent by acquiring the costly Trident . . . . (7:297)

The only remaining longer range theater nuclear weapons would be the small number of US weapons allocated to longer range strike aircraft based principally in Great Britain on aging FB-111 aircraft. The likelihood that these early-generation aircraft could penetrate improved Soviet air defenses is quite low. The new US tactical fighter, the F-15E, could be helpful.(2:4)

In sum, modernization of NATO's nuclear forces will be controversial. There are three conceivable means to increase NATO's nuclear capabilities: (1) a nuclear Lance missile replacement; (2) a new nuclear-armed aircraft delivering air-to-surface missile (called the TASM); and (3) an increase in the number of nuclear artillery shells.

In the short term, the only real option open to NATO is to increase the number and capability of nuclear-armed fighter aircraft and to introduce a medium-range nuclear air-to-surface missile (ASM) for them. Nuclear capable fighter aircraft are not as controversial as artillery or short-range missiles, and numerous modernization programs are underway to bolster the fighter force. Although they are vulnerable on the ground and must penetrate Soviet air defenses, fighter aircraft would provide the flexibility to execute both short- and long-range nuclear strikes, a feature attractive to nuclear war planners. Some would argue that fighters should not be used to deliver these weapons—some other aircraft should be used.

15

In the long-term, NATO should focus on maintaining a smaller, modernized force of tactical nuclear weapons and on bolstering its long-range nuclear systems which are not covered by the INF Treaty. Such a program, if successfully implemented, would restore theater nuclear deterrence and would stop any slide toward further denuclearization.

Some of the west European allies fear that the removal of US medium-range nuclear weapons from their territory is the first phase of reduction in America's defense commitment to Europe. Article V of the 1949 North Atlantic Treaty requires the allies to defend one another from aggression. Furthermore, the presence of more than 300,000 US servicemen and their dependents and about 1,000,000 Americans all together in Europe guarantees the US military commitment. On the other hand, the future of US forces in Europe is in doubt. A number of factors seem to be converging on behalf of a sizeable reduction in the American force presence in Europe by the end of the century. These factors include:

-- mounting political pressures on the US defense budget,

-- growing demands on US Armed Forces in the Persian Gulf and other places outside the NATO area,

-- rising public and congressional anger over what is perceived to be Europe's continued unwillingness to bear its fair share of the common defense burden, and

-- continuation of a comparative disinvestment in conventional force modernization and expansion.[7:297]

16

For that reason, western European allies, especially
those that enjoy sizeable trade surpluses, must shoulder a
greater share of the burden of defending Europe. On the other
hand, the United States should not reduce its troops in Europe
until the allies proceed with conventional modernization.

Conventional Modernization and Arms Control

The removal of intermediate-range nuclear weapons from
Europe has not suddenly created a conventional gap in NATO's
defense posture; rather, it has magnified the existing
conventional imbalance between NATO and Warsaw Pact and
heightened the need to redress it. Based on the most recent
compilation by the International Institute of Strategic Studies,
the Pact has a two-to-one advantage in main battle tanks,
three-to-one in artillery shells, two-to-one in attack
helicopters, and four-to-one in fighter-interceptor aircraft.
Overall equality in the number of active duty and reserve
personnel that both alliances can mobilize obscures the
disparity in numbers on the central front, where the Pact has
concentrated it best fighting forces.[8:237]

Is NATO actually inferior to the Warsaw Pact? As you
see, the Warsaw Pact enjoys a quantitative superiority over NATO
in both manpower and most components of conventional weaponry.
But the numbers alone can be misleading and cannot by themselves
answer basic questions about the relative capabilities of each
side's forces to perform their required missions. The quality
and quantity of forces vary from one region to another. Most

17

European defense analysts believe that NATO is qualitatively superior to the Warsaw Pact and is capable of defending itself against a Soviet attack. NATO has some problems, nonetheless. Current ammunition stockpiles would last less than 30 days under a full-scale Soviet attack versus anticipated 90 days for the Pact. Readiness and mobilization times are still inadequate. The interoperability of guns, ammunition, and radio communications from country to country is poor to nonexistent. Finally, there remains a very important inability to distinguish friendly from enemy aircraft.

There is another important aspect of the INF Treaty's direct and unfavorable impact on NATO's conventional defenses. The treaty's ban of all ground-based, intermediate-range ballistic and cruise missile impairs NATO from implementing its declared Follow-on Forces Attack (FOFA) strategy, which calls for deep interdiction strikes using conventional munitions on Soviet air bases, communications centers, and advanced ground reinforcement echelons. The US Army's Tactical Missile System (ATACMS) is a better alternative. It is a conventionally armed, highly accurate missile whose projected 200 kilometers range makes it an effective weapon for follow-on forces attack.[5:38]

Allied military planners certainly recognize the need to correct these deficiencies and to modernize NATO's conventional forces. Conventional modernization, however, is an expensive proposition. "Of NATO's 16 nations only Italy, Luxemburg, Norway, and Turkey plan to increase real defense

18

spending in 1988."[7:296] Future modernization is likely to be economically even more onerous for the allies.

It is my opinion that NATO is highly unlikely to make the conventional force improvements seemingly dictated by the INF Treaty. This leaves open only one road to redress the non-nuclear military balance in Europe: reduction of the Soviet threat. The Kremlin leadership has surely made this calculation, and thus, Mr Gorbachev's announcement at the United Nations on 7 December 1988 declared this policy to the world. He announced plans to unilaterally withdraw 8 divisions, 10,000 tanks, 8,500 artillery pieces, and 800 combat aircraft from the European military theater while reducing the total number of Soviet men in uniform by 500,000 men.[9:1]

Conventional arms control has long been overshadowed by START negotiations and by the completion of the INF Treaty. But that is now changing. NATO will offer proposals drastically cutting the number of tanks in Europe to 40,000 and seeking to reshape NATO and Warsaw Pact forces into a more stable, defensive military posture. The NATO proposals, to be unveiled in Vienna at the next talks on conventional arms control, are a response to Mr Gorbachev's announcement. The western proposals would apply to both sides and would not be undertaken unilaterally.[9:1]

Under the NATO plan, ceilings would be set for the number of main battle weapons in Europe and would include limits on armaments that could be stationed in "the heavy traffic zone" of central Europe. This zone concept is a new definition of a broad region in Europe where the two armies deploy the bulk of their forces, where the majority of the fighting would be expected in case of a land war and into which reinforcements would first be sent. This proposal precludes a cosmetic pullback of forces from a more narrowly defined "central front" where the two alliances face off along the West German border.[9:1]

Under the NATO plan, all heavy equipment above the limit would have to be withdrawn to such a distance that it could not be redeployed quickly in time of war. At least 20 percent of the overall limits for weapons under negotiation would be outside this central zone, according to the NATO plan. For example, of the 40,000 tanks allowed to remain in Europe under the NATO proposal, 8,000 would have to be outside the central zone. This proposal was particularly controversial among the NATO ministers, because of fears of leaving the impression that Norway, Greece, and Turkey were left hanging loosely along the alliance's boundary. The issue is still not settled.[9:1]

Currently, according to NATO, Western armies in Europe field 16,424 tanks while the Soviet Union has 37,000 and its Warsaw Pact allies have 14,500. The future 40,000 figure would be roughly split between NATO and Warsaw Pact tanks, although the issue is a bit sticky because France and Spain are members of NATO while not integrating their militaries into it.[9:1]

While conventional parity is being achieved, however, nuclear deterrence will continue to form an essential part of NATO's defensive posture and thus, must be preserved as an effective force even within the restrictions of the INF Treaty.

Achieving parity in conventional military capability between Warsaw Pact and the NATO allies will require very delicate negotiations over a period of years. Parity in conventional military capability is not to be confused with mutual or balanced force reductions as they are commonly understood--determining a military parity between the antagonists requires a very careful analysis of every country's military forces, their equipment, training, doctrine, ammunition stocks, interoperability, etc. If NATO and the Warsaw Pact can achieve conventional military parity by some means, then it follows both sides will rely less on their nuclear arsenals to deter one another. Reducing reliance on nuclear weapons diminishes their importance to each side, thus eventually large reductions in these weapons should be possible.

CHAPTER IV

THE IMPACT OF THE INF TREATY ON

TURKEY'S DEFENSE REQUIREMENTS

<u>Turkey's Defense Policy</u>

The Turkish Republic has chosen to tie its foreign policy to its great leader Ataturk's well-known doctrine: "peace at home, peace in the world," since her inception. The essence of Turkish foreign policy is to most effectively protect national interests, contribute to peace in the region, and the world in line with the fundamental principles set by great Ataturk. The continuity of the state is the keystone of Turkey's foreign policy concept.

The Turkish Armed Forces are responsible for defending the country, nation, state, and to fulfil their duties within the NATO framework. The aim of the Turkish Armed Forces is to upgrade its armaments to the level of the NATO standards in order to defend national independence and to realize the requirements of a joint defense system within the NATO framework. Today the main threat to Turkey is the Soviet Union and its clients--Bulgaria and Romania. The Turkish Armed Forces must be able to first deter invasion; second, deter nuclear weapons first use (a joint objective hostage to NATO support); third, hold the Warsaw Pact or other invaders until reinforcement forces come then repel the enemy.

Nuclear Weapons

Nuclear capability plays a critical role in the
strategy of flexible response, as well as in deterrence. NATO
and Warsaw Pact missile forces (less INF) have a very limited
tactical depth. The Soviets' SS-21 has a 120 kilometers range
and NATO's counterpart, the Lance, has a 70 kilometers range.
These missiles are much like nuclear artillery, in that they
have a limited nuclear deterrence value. On the other hand, as
I mentioned earlier, their use will be problematic. The Turkish
Air Force has the ability to deliver nuclear bombs. This
capability provides more a powerful nuclear deterrence that the
short-range weapons do, but is not sufficient to offset the loss
of the INF weapons. These Turkish fighters would provide the
flexibility to execute both short- and long-range nuclear
strikes. Moreover, Turkey can launch nuclear strikes targeting
to the north of the Black Sea coast, known as the soft belly of
Russia. The Soviets are potentially vulnerable to air attacks
from the south, where Soviet industrial regions are exposed and
critical lines of communication supporting Soviet forces in
eastern Europe are vulnerable. Turkey with her 32 airfields,
can be seen as a gigantic aircraft carrier strategically
positioned in the region.

In short term, any modernization of NATO's nuclear
forces will be controversial. The only possible option to NATO
is to increase the number and capability of nuclear armed
fighter aircraft available for the NATO Air Forces, and to

23

introduce a medium-range nuclear ASM for them. Medium-range
nuclear ASMs can be a better option for Turkey. Furthermore,
NATO's new General Political Guidelines state "nuclear weapons
will be developed and deployed to implement the new long-range
employment doctrine: Theater Nuclear Forces modernization in
Europe has shifted the weight of regional nuclear armaments and
target options away from the battlefield towards the adversary's
side with a t.. ' , of shifting deep in Warsaw Pact
territory."[2:5]

In terms of the short-range nuclear missiles, the
future is more important than today. Because, if both sides
upgrade their tactical missile forces with increased ranges
approaching the 500 kilometers, Turkey will remain mostly within
the reach of new short-range missiles. Like other NATO members,
Turkey has no anti-missile system. Turkey will need to
modernize its air defense systems and these systems must be dual
capable--anti-air/anti-missile.

A careful review of the Turkish nuclear weapons
capability discloses some weaknesses which need correction to
redress the imbalance caused by the INF Treaty. Not only will
Turkey require upgraded missile batteries and dual capable
aircraft with both nuclear and conventional weapon capability,
she will need to invest in all the requisite infrastructure as
well. Since the international political climate between NATO
and the Warsaw Pact is very calm and relatively free from crises
now (and should remain so for several years while the Soviet

24

Union gets its economic house in order), the pressure to modernize Turkey's nuclear forces is greatly reduced. The long lead time for this modernization and its reduced relative importance argue against assigning this task the highest modernization priority--it should fall below conventional force modernization to counter the greater threat from the Warsaw Pact conventional forces.

Another factor to consider when prioritizing defense needs is the fact that Turkey does not actually control the nuclear weapons which her forces would use. They remain under the control of the United States. So, nuclear systems cannot be considered to be one of Turkey's basic defense systems. Moreover, like the INF Treaty has done, a treaty may be signed by the United States and USSR which may remove all short-range nuclear weapons from NATO and Warsaw Pact countries. Turkey cannot control this process.

Conventional Force Comparisons

By reducing the nuclear component of the superpowers' arsenals in Europe, the INF Treaty has focused attention on conventional forces. Although the conventional forces are not able to provide deterrence as well as the nuclear forces, they serve to provide stability. Turkey military effectiveness should be examined within the framework of NATO's southern region. NATO contingency plans provide for three land combat theaters: northeast Italy, Greek-Turkish Thrace, and eastern Turkey. The fourth potential combat theater, the Mediterranean

Sea, links the other three. The constraining geography,
combined with the limited capability of local forces, makes
mutual support among the combat areas extremely difficult. The
features of the military balance in the two land theaters as
follows:

> Northern Greece - Turkish Thrace: The equivalent of 34
> Soviet, Romanian, and Bulgarian divisions are available in
> the area. These forces are largely mechanized and are
> equipped with a total of 6,750 tanks and over 6,400
> artillery and mortar pieces. They are on terrain suitable
> for armored offensive operations and could be reinforced by
> amphibious forces and by airborne/air mobile divisions. Of
> the 34 divisions, the equivalent of just 22 divisions with
> 3,680 tanks and 2,940 artillery and mortar pieces are either
> deployed forward or are maintained at high states of
> readiness. NATO's 25 Greek and Turkish divisions in the
> area are mainly infantry. Turkey and Greece together have
> 3,000 tanks and 2,800 artillery/mortar pieces. (10:21)

> Eastern Turkey - There are 20 Soviet divisions which could
> be committed against the area equipped with about 4,300
> tanks and over 4,800 artillery pieces. Of this number, just
> over 12 divisions with 2,435 tanks and 2,735 artillery
> pieces are deployed forward. These forces could be
> reinforced by the airborne and air assault/mobile divisions
> and by amphibious forces. Turkish Army retains eight
> divisions in northeast Turkey. Four more divisions in
> southeast Turkey are for use there to protect its extensive
> borders, but would be available for defense against the
> Warsaw Pact. Turkey has 1,000 tanks and 1,800 artillery
> pieces in this region. (10:22)

The flexibility of air forces renders separate regional
comparisons difficult. The air balance in the southern region
shows 615 fighter-bomber aircraft available to NATO against 695
for Warsaw Pact. The interceptor asymmetry is significant,
however, with NATO deploying 259 planes against 1,560 for the
Warsaw Pact. The range of some of the Warsaw Pact aircraft is
such that they have the potential to operate anywhere in the

Mediterranean Sea, endangering the security of sea lines of communication.[10:22]

In terms of the naval balance, simple numerical comparisons of types of ships do not tell the full story. The naval balance may be more usefully compared in terms the abilities of the naval forces of NATO and the Warsaw Pact to accomplish their respective missions in the face of opposition by the other side. In the southern region, maritime forces' task is to support the land and air forces, and maintain the sea lines of communication in the Mediterranean in the face of the Soviet Mediterranean Squadron. They also have the task of securing the Turkish and Gibraltar Straits, in order to deny the Soviet Black Sea fleet access to the Mediterranean Sea and to guarantee the flow of reinforcements and resupplies to NATO's southern region. It can be said that NATO naval forces have the ability to accomplish these missions. But, there is an important point that since the Soviet Union's first priority objective will be the Turkish Straits, the attack will involve amphibious operations. This necessitates a strategic defense capability in depth, in echelons, beginning from enemy coasts at the Black Sea.

As you see, the force comparison is not favorable to NATO and Turkey. But, the mountainous structure of Turkey will be helpful for Turkish Armed Forces in order to defend their country against numerically superior enemy. This mountainous structure of terrain gives Turkey the advantage of being a

27

strong resistance region. This advantage alone will cause an aggressor to lose time and strength. On the other hand, geography creates two vulnerable areas of openings in the west and east of the country. The vulnerable area in the west is the Turkish Straits and the vulnerable area in the east is the plateau of Erzurum. Any invasion launched from the north can be stopped if adequate forces are deployed to these areas. As a result, it can be said that the Turkish Armed Forces are sufficient to defend the country against a Warsaw Pact attack until reinforcements come. But that is only currently true, provided Turkey can depend on the United States to implement the necessary measures to execute the full-range of the NATO flexible response strategy. Modernizing Turkish forces is a high priority item because of the time required, the vast cost involved, and the complex technologies which must be learned.

By reducing the role and number of theater nuclear weapons, the INF Treaty increases the escalation and general nuclear war probability. The best way to lower dependence on nuclear weapons and to reduce the probability of their early use is to build an adequate conventional force. Conventional stability talks may be helpful for Turkey. If any agreement provides credible cuts in Warsaw Pact forces, Turkish Armed Forces' level will become more sufficient. But Turkey must be very cautious about new NATO proposals because Turkey has a unique situation. Among her six neighbors, Turkey has only border with only one of her allies (Greece). Besides the Warsaw

Pact countries, Turkey is bordered by mostly other unstable neighbors. Turkey must therefore maintain a credible armed force to protect her rights and interests not only against the Warsaw Pact, but these unstable countries as well.

Modernization Requirements

1. **Land Forces:** The Turkish Land Forces consist of a Headquarters, four Army Commands, an independent Corps Command, and two Interior Zone Commands. Ninety percent of the Turkish land forces are NATO-assigned units which consist of 14 divisions, 18 brigades, and an independent regiment. The remaining Turkish Armed Forces are committed in "other forces for NATO" status. As major supplements of the land forces, the Turkish First Army is deployed in Thrace, the Straits, and the Kocaeli region; the Second Army in the southeast Anatolia; the Third Army in eastern Anatolia in order to defend their respective areas of responsibility. The Aegean Army coordinates and controls the training units and centers exclusively for these major elements and other units.

In terms of the land warfare, the mountainous structure of Turkey and the inadequate railway and highway networks have negative effects on strategic movements, rapidity, flexibility, and the economy of forces. For that reason, every army has to defend its area mostly by itself. This situation is why Turkey has maintained such a large land force.

For the Land Forces, it is necessary to acquire modern equipment and weapons for intelligence, mobility, firepower,

29

command-control-communication, and combat service support. Considering the defensive operations in Thrace, armored power and anti-tank capability should be increased because defense in this region is rendered difficult by the narrowness of the area between the border and the Straits and the lack of the natural obstacles.

To increase the fire power of the field artillery target acquisition and damage assessment systems, weapon systems, ammunition, and command-control systems should be acquired. In order to enhance the Short-Range Air Defense (SHORAD) capabilities, 35 mm Oerlikon anti-aircraft guns and STINGER missiles production projects should be started. Adverse weather and night fighting capabilities should be increased.

2. Navy: The Turkish Navy consists of four main sub-commands: Fleet Command, Sea Area Command North, Sea Area Command South, and Naval Training Command. The Turkish Navy consists of 6 modernized destroyers, 8 older destroyers, 16 submarines, 26 minesweepers, 13 minelayers, 4 frigates, 15 FACs (missiles), 10 FACs (torpedo), 29 FACs (gun), 6 landing vessels (over 1,000 tons), and 88 landing vessels (below 1,000 tons).

The Soviet amphibious offensive in the Black Sea can only be stopped by a defense from the Soviet coasts up to the beaches on both sides of Bosphorus. This mission can be accomplished by an adequate navy and air force. Considering the tasks, in both the Mediterranean Sea and the Black Sea, the primary objectives of the Turkish Navy's reinforcement and modernization program should be the replacement of conventional destroyers with modern guided missile frigates and destroyers; submarine and guided missile patrol craft construction; modernization of the early warning systems; procurement of modern maritime patrol aircraft and helicopters; establishment of a naval base in the eastern Mediterranean to be used by the Turkish Navy and allied naval forces; and modernization of the command and control system.

3. Air Forces: Nineteen squadrons of the Turkish Air Force are assigned to NATO, of which three are reserved for transportation and 16 for combat missions, consisting of various types of aircraft such as F-5s, F-4s, and F-104s. The Turkish Air Force Command subunits are: 1st and 2nd Tactical Air Force Commands, Air Training Command, Air Transportation Main Base Command, and Supply and Maintenance Centers.

The vulnerability of borders and difficulties of communication in Turkey restrict or may even prevent during war possibility of economy of forces in favor of a certain front. This disadvantage can be neutralized especially by building up the strength and the capability of the Turkish Air Forces, so that they can allocate a sustainable level of effort to support ground operations starting from the beginning of the war. Being well aware of the importance of the Air Force, Turkey concluded an agreement with the United States for the co-production of 160 F-16 C/D aircraft in Turkey. These aircraft shall enter service in the early 1990s.

The air defense of Turkey, is especially important for NATO as well. It is very closely interrelated with the overall air defense of Mediterranean. If Turkey's air space is not properly defended, then almost all the Soviet air assets will be free to jeopardize the air security of the Mediterranean, including COMSIXTHFLT. If Turkey's air defense is not fully robust and capable, then the Sixth Fleet will have to allocate more air assets for the air defense role and this will reduce its anticipated air strike power. For these reasons, Turkish Air Force air defense weapons, missiles, and reporting/control systems should be modernized and reinforced.[11:14]

Airlift capacity is another important subject. Those C-47 aircraft which have already completed their economic lives should be replaced by new light transport aircraft. In addition, reconnaissance and intelligence systems should be renewed. Command-control-communication systems, maintenance centers, and supply systems should be modernized.

Funds for Modernization

In order to continue her national existence and strengthen her defense, Turkey does not hesitate in setting aside 20 percent of her national budget for National Defense. Besides the national budget and allied military aid, "The Defense Industry Support Fund" (DIDA) which was established in November 1985, will be available for the Armed Forces' modernization efforts and the realization of main projects. Revenue sources of the fund are sound, widespread, free from

32

conjunctural changes of the economy, and not limited to the annual fiscal cycles. DIDA has taken over some projects dealing with the Turkish Armed Forces' requirements. Those are:

- armored combat vehicles,
- multiple launch rocket system,
- mobile radar complex,
- low-level air defense system,
- helicopters,
- HF/SSB wireless system, and
- light transport aircraft.

CHAPTER V

FINDINGS

1. By eliminating those theater nuclear weapons having the most deterrent value, the INF Treaty causes the NATO's strategy of flexible response to lose credibility.

2. Any modernization of NATO's nuclear forces will be controversial. In the short term, the only real option open to NATO is to increase the number and capability of nuclear-armed fighter aircraft and to introduce a medium-range nuclear air-to-surface missile for them. In the long term, NATO should focus on maintaining a smaller, modernized force of tactical nuclear weapons and on bolstering its long-range nuclear systems which are not covered by the INF Treaty. Such a program would restore theater deterrence credibility and capability.

3. Despite European concerns that the INF Treaty will serve to decouple the US strategic deterrent from Europe's defense by eliminating equitable nuclear risk-sharing among alliance members, the presence of more than 300,000 US servicemen in Europe guarantees the US military commitment to the NATO strategy for the next 5 years.

4. NATO should not plan for a significant reduction of the Soviet threat. Mr Gorbachev could fall or he could be forced by economic failure or internal power struggles to a return to hostility toward the west. The Soviet Union will continue its efforts to politically divide the allies.

5. The threat to Turkey is greater than it was. The Turkish Straits are the starting points for Soviet intentions over the region. The increasing importance of the Mediterranean Sea and the Middle East will undoubtedly cause the Soviet pressures on Turkey to increase.

6. In the NATO's southern region, the conventional force comparison does not favor NATO and Turkey. Turkish Armed Forces are sufficient to defend the country against Warsaw Pact attack only within the framework of the previous flexible response strategy, but require extensive modernization to remain competitive under the new agreement.

7. The Conventional Stability Talks between NATO and the Warsaw Pact may be helpful for Turkey. If any agreement provides credible cuts in Warsaw Pact forces, Turkish Armed Forces' size will become more sufficient. Turkey must be very cautious about NATO proposals because of her unstable neighbors, however. Turkey must maintain a credible armed forces to protect her rights and interests not only against Warsaw Pact, but these unstable countries as well.

8. On the nuclear side, by considering the potential battle areas and the threat, Turkey requires modern nuclear capable aircraft (which she does not now have) far more than short-range nuclear missiles (which are not now based in Turkey) and nuclear artillery (which is). Modern medium-range air-to-surface missiles (nuclear and conventional) could reinforce the Turkish Air Force's nuclear capability.

9. Both sides should soon begin modernizing their short-range missile forces within the parameters of the treaty. If so, Turkey will remain mostly within the reach of these missiles. Turkey will need to modernize its air defense systems to have dual capability against missiles or aircraft.

10. Considering the defensive operation in Thrace, armored unit strength and anti-tank capability should be increased.

11. The Turkish Navy should be reinforced and modernized in order to defend against the modern Soviet naval combatants, aircraft, and missiles threatening NATO's strategic control of the Turkish Straits.

12. The air defense of Turkey is especially important not only for Turkey, but for NATO as well. If Turkey's air space is not properly defended, then almost all the Soviet air assets will be free to jeopardize the air security of the Mediterranean Sea.

13. Turkey's geography and lack of a well developed internal transportation network commit Turkey to maintain large forces propositioned at critical border areas. Since the Turkish Air Force can operate effectively throughout the country independently of ground transportation limits, it can provide extremely valuable force multiplication, power projection, and critical air defense to assist commanders in defeating or deterring enemy attack. This highly mobile and flexible force, if increased sufficiently with modern equipment, would provide a very cost effective means for Turkey to buildup its conventional force capability.

CHAPTER VI

RECOMMENDATIONS

1. Turkey should give first priority to modernize its
conventional forces.

2. Among the services, Turkey should give first priority to
modernize the Air Force. The modernization should emphasize
dual capable aircraft which can be used for both nuclear and
conventional missions and should also include development of a
robust air defense system which can defend targets against both
conventional and nuclear weapons delivered by aircraft or
missiles.

Turkey in the Region: Background
Regional Assessment

The Republic of Turkey is located between Asia and Europe, covering an area of 780,000 square kilometers, with a population of approximately 55,000,000. In addition to its situation of close proximity to the western and eastern blocs, and the Middle East countries, it also controls one of the most important sea routes. All these geographical factors, membership of the NATO Alliance, and long-term relationships with the Middle East countries give Turkey a special geostrategical importance.

The NATO front extends from the North Cape in Norway to Mount Agri in eastern Turkey, with a total length of approximately 3,600 miles. The width of NATO's central region is only about 500 miles, with the remainder of NATO's territory constituting the two flanks. NATO's southern region, covering about 470,000 square miles, includes the Mediterranean Sea and provides a geographical approach toward southwestern USSR.

NATO's southern flank is integrally related to the Middle East, which in turn, abuts western Europe on one side and Africa on the other. In addition to being a potential bread basket of global significance, the Middle East and the north African/Mediterranean littoral are the world's most important providers of petroleum.

The Middle East is not a geographic unit like "western Europe" or not even like the "Balkans" where countries share

38

certain similar geographic peculiarities and where they are not placed far away from each other. In the Middle East, on the other hand, countries like Iran and Algeria have apparently very little in common as far as geography is concerned. The Middle East comprises countries belonging to North Africa, the eastern Mediterranean, and the Persian Gulf subregions. There are, therefore, at least three subdivisions within the region. The Middle East is not a politically coherent, tightly-knit unit like "western Europe" where the countries share certain political characteristics such as systems of government, culture, and modernization of social institutions and where all levels of society share a modern view of the future and have common aspiration for economic and educational development. In the Middle East, to the contrary, there are "republics" with democratic and totalitarian regimes, as well as modernizing and conservative monarchies. There are also countries with differing political loyalties. Those allied to the west, to the east, and those trying to adopt a nonaligned line, make up the Middle East "mosaic." The Middle East is not an economic unit, either. Petroleum-rich and petroleum-poor countries on one hand and countries with advanced and backward infrastructures on the other, exist side by side. Culturally and ethnically, however, Islam is the nearly universal religion and Arabs are the predominant ethnic group, and these two characteristics may be considered as the only common denominators leaving Turkey, Israel, and Iran out. As a result, the Turkish and Iranian

39

plateaus have traditionally formed separate power centers independent of the Arab world. At present and for the foreseeable future, Ankara, Teheran, Cairo, and Tel Aviv seem to be the most prominent subregional power centers.

By virtue of its crucial location, the Mediterranean Sea links NATO's southern flank with the Middle East in a single geopolitical entity and serves as the maritime lifeline of NATO's southern region. The Mediterranean Sea, where the three continents of the World Island (Africa, Europe, and Asia) meet has historically been a target of competition between major powers seeking to dominate this strategic region. Today there are 16 states that have coasts directly on the Mediterranean Sea. As we observe the political spectrum of the Mediterranean Sea, we realize that it is quite wide and in the last half century it has changed drastically. While the northern coasts of the Mediterranean Sea are shared by five NATO states, its southern and eastern coasts are shared by mostly unstable countries. These developments create a greater power vacuum and more risks to the western Europeans than they did several decades ago.

In short, geography and history have combined to make this region a strategic hub of worldwide significance. All natural routes--land, sea, and air--from the Black Sea to the Mediterranean Sea, and from the Balkans to the Persian Gulf, lead across Turkey and, in most cases in one way or another, cross the Strait's area.

Appendix 1

The southern region is, and will continue to be, a key factor in the broader context of US global strategy to restrict Soviet expansion to the south. The Mediterranean Sea will remain an area of major concern for the Soviets. Along the sea's northern littoral, the Soviets wish to divide NATO. In the south, the aim is to strengthen relationships with Soviet proxies (e.g., Libya and Syria) in an effort to rebuild its own regional strategic relationships after the loss of key bases and facilities in Egypt.

A number of factors converge to demand greater attention to southern flank security: (1) a persistent and steady Soviet naval buildup in the Mediterranean that threatens to hold the allied Mediterranean force--now reduced in size due to increased US deployments in the Indian Ocean--at risk; (2) political struggles between Greece and Turkey that impede effective military coordination in the event of a serious external threat; (3) electoral trends in several states (notably Greece and Spain) that suggest at least a questioning--if not a rejection--of NATO membership and/or the continued presence of US military bases on their soil; (4) a command structure that, due principally to political and communication factors, will frustrate a coordinated theater defense; and (5) the potentially vital role of southern flank states in a regional conflict that originates as an out-of-area crisis.

These factors all tend to constrain (or in some cases prevent) the region's contribution to NATO and, therefore,

41

western policies designed to ameliorate these unfavorable trends must be sensitive to the relationship between domestic crises and regional strategic decline.

These problems combine to reduce the regional strategic cohesion of the southern flank which invites Soviet political-military pressure against key western-aligned states. This, in turn, could encourage the embryonic, but politically significant, pacifist movements that urge southern Europe (particularly the Spanish and Greek electorates) to reject NATO membership and ultimately any US presence in the region.

The USSR aims to establish itself as a major power in the Mediterranean/Middle East region; to reduce western, and especially American, influence in the area; to counter and/or neutralize the US strategic posture; and to secure access routes to the oceans. A prerequisite for all these goals is easy access for the Soviet Black Sea Fleet into the Mediterranean Sea through the Turkish Straits.

The growing Soviet military presence in the Mediterranean, created by penetration into the Arab countries, must be taken as part of an overall Soviet maneuver aiming to outflank Europe. Therefore, any examination of the problems menacing NATO's southern flank must be made against the background of that growing Soviet presence, its causes, and its implications as they affect every country in the area. A combination of Soviet naval power and Arab oil can be used as an instrument of pressure to isolate western Europe from America,

Appendix 1

and to neutralize and finally destroy its defensive alliance.
The prospect of being able to shut-off Gulf oil to the west is a
major impetus to Soviet global strategy. Consequently, the Red
Navy is endeavoring to build a systems of bases along the tanker
routes from the Persian Gulf. The eastern Mediterranean/Middle
East is only the stepping stone for this thrust. As the Soviet
stake in the Suez Canal and the Persian Gulf increases, pressure
for full Soviet control of the Turkish Straits is likely to
mount.

Turkey's Geographical Position

· Turkey is at once a Balkan, an east European, a
Mediterranean, and a Middle Eastern country. It is the only
NATO member other than Norway to share a border with the USSR,
and the Soviet-Turkish border is much longer of the two. There
are other ways in which Turkey's strategic location makes it a
vitally important member of the western camp. Turkey controls
the crucial Bosphorus and Dardanelles Straits, as well as
strategically vital air space. It enjoys a dominating position
over the eastern Mediterranean. It lies on historic invasion
routes to and from the Middle East and eastern Mediterranean
regions, and on the shortest axes leading to the warm seas that
have been targets of Russian striving for centuries. The
country constitutes a bridge not only between east and west, but
also between the affluent north and the developing south.
Perhaps most significantly, the world's greatest known oil
reserves lie just beyond Turkey. The position of Turkey is so

important that, in the words of a well-known statesman, it is virtually a firebreak, a firewall between the Middle East and the Communist world.

Turkey has a total length of 2,735 kilometers of boundaries with her 6 neighboring countries. They are: USSR 610, Bulgaria 269, Greece 212, Syria 877, Iraq 331, and Iran 454 kilometers. The total length of Turkish coasts along the Black Sea, the Sea of Marmara, the Aegean Sea, and the Mediterranean Sea is 8,272 kilometers. The relative position of Turkey's borders and coasts confronts her with a more critical and vulnerable situation than her allies. That is to say, Turkey has the longest direct border with USSR. In case of war, this border of 610 kilometers may increase to 1,064 kilometers with the inclusion of the Iranian border of 454 kilometers. In Thrace, Turkey has a border with the loyal satellite of USSR, Bulgaria, and in the south she has bordered with Syria and Iraq which receive aid from USSR and are mostly unstable countries. In addition to common borders, the Black Sea coast has to be defended against Soviet, Bulgarian, and Rumanian naval forces. In other words, among her six neighbors, Turkey has a border with only one of her allies--Greece. Turkey's situation cannot be compared even with that of West Germany, which has borders with Denmark, the Netherlands, Belgium, Luxemburg, and France all who are members of NATO. Even with her ally Greece, Turkey has bilateral problems, some of which appear to be intractable. However, the process of reconciliation has started since the

Appendix 1

Davos meeting of the Greek and Turkish prime ministers on
31 January 1988.[12:71]   On the other hand, the superpowers'
struggle has continued in the Balkans.   In recent years, Romania
and Bulgaria have led the way in promoting regional disarmament
advocating the establishment of nuclear and chemical-free zones
in the Balkans.   Turkey holds the view that arms control in
Europe should not be treated in regional terms, divorced from
the unique strategic realities of the continent.   It is doubtful
that such regional approaches can lead to enhanced security and
stability which, essentially, is the purpose of arms control and
disarmament.   In the absence of general and comprehensive
solutions, regional approaches may easily develop into pockets
of vulnerability and gaps of security.   Greece, for example,
along with Romania and Bulgaria, advocates forming a nuclear
free zone in the Balkans.

Appendix 1

DEFENCE OF SOUTHERN REGION

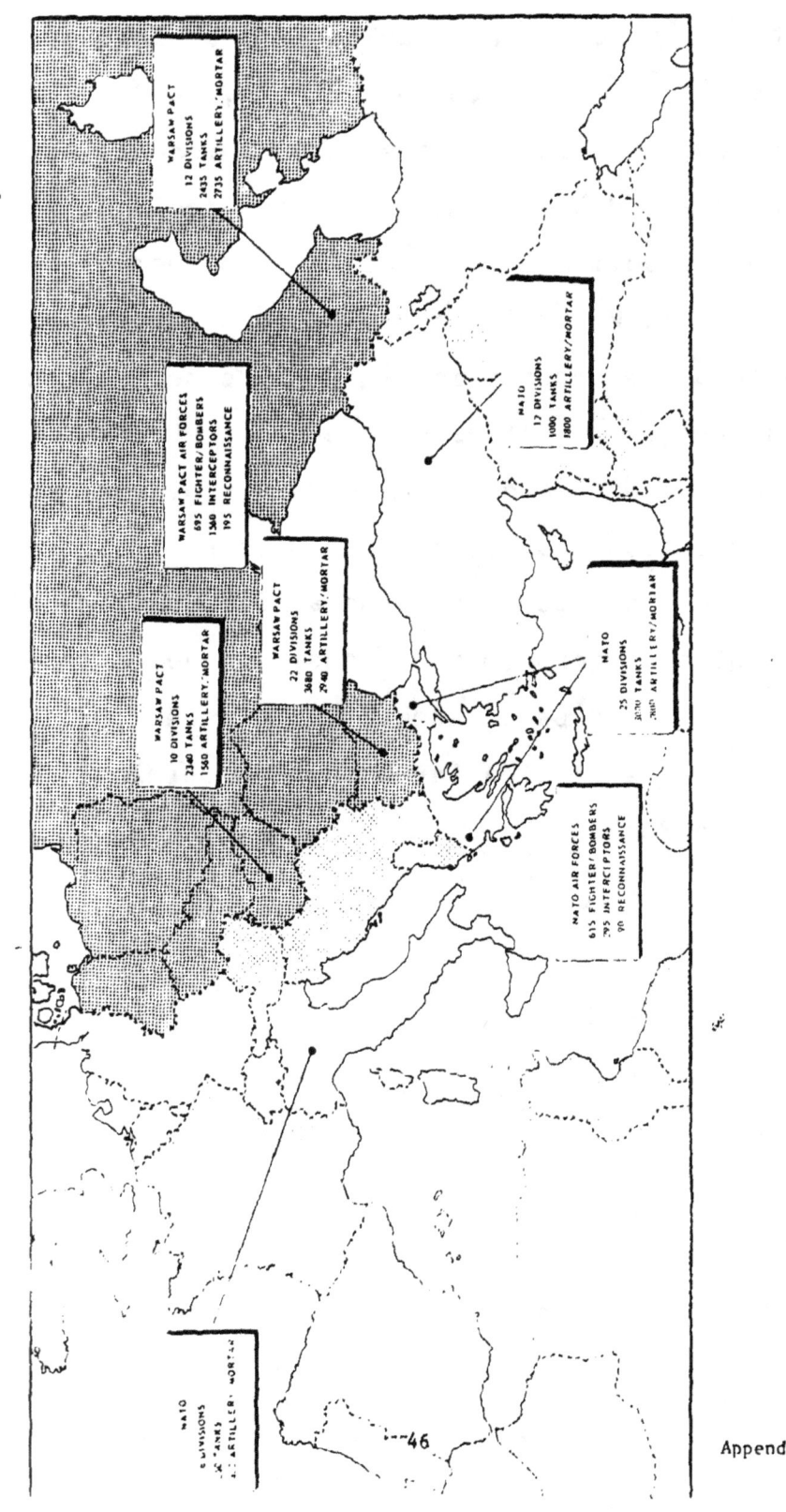

WARSAW PACT
12 DIVISIONS
2435 TANKS
2735 ARTILLERY/MORTAR

WARSAW PACT AIR FORCES
695 FIGHTER/BOMBERS
1360 INTERCEPTORS
195 RECONNAISSANCE

WARSAW PACT
22 DIVISIONS
3680 TANKS
2940 ARTILLERY/MORTAR

WARSAW PACT
10 DIVISIONS
2240 TANKS
1560 ARTILLERY/MORTAR

NATO
17 DIVISIONS
1000 TANKS
1800 ARTILLERY/MORTAR

NATO
25 DIVISIONS
3170 TANKS
2900 ARTILLERY/MORTAR

NATO AIR FORCES
615 FIGHTER/BOMBERS
395 INTERCEPTORS
90 RECONNAISSANCE

NATO
6 DIVISIONS
52 TANKS
45 ARTILLERY/MORTAR

-46-

LIST OF REFERENCES

1. "Negotiating the INF Treaty." Department of State Bulletin: March 1988.

2. "US Nuclear Weapon Programme." Maxwell AFB AL: Air War College Resident Studies, DS 613.

3. Editorial Research Reports. December 24, 1987.

4. "NATO Information Service Brussels." NATO Handbook: April 1986.

5. Santis, Hugh de. "After INF: The Political-Military Landscape of Europe." The Washington Quarterly: Summer 1988.

6. Snyder, Jed C. "European Security After the INF Treaty, The World and I." August 1988

7. Record, Jeffrey and David B. Rivkin, Jr. "Defending post-INF Europe, Foreign Affairs." Spring 1988.

8. "The Military Balance, 1988/89." London: The International Institute for Strategic Studies, 1988.

9. Shanker, Thom. "Allies Answers Soviet Cuts." Chicago: Chicago Tribune, 22 December 1988.

10. "NATO and Warsaw Pact Force Comparisons." Brussels: NATO Information Service, 1984.

11. Biren, Isik. "NATO's Security in the Mediterranean.: Ankara, Turkey: Turkish Review Quarterly Digest, Winter, 1987.

12. Joint Statement by Prime Minister Turgut Ozal and Greek Prime Minister Andreas Papandreau. Ankara, Turkey: Turkish Review Quarterly Digest, Spring 1988.

BIBLIOGRAPHY

Biren, Isik. "NATO's Security in the Mediterranean." Turkish Review Quarterly Digest, Winter 1987, Ankara.

Cooper, Marry H. "Defending Europe." Editorial Research Reports, December 24, 1987.

Crowe, William J. "Why the Joint Chiefs Support the INF Treaty." Arms Control Today, April 1988.

"Defence and Economics in Turkey." NATO's Sixteen Nations, September 1986, Brussel.

Erdem, Vahit. "Defense Industry and Investment Projects." Turkish Review Quarterly Digest, Spring 1988, Ankara.

Forsberg, Randall. "INF: A First Step Toward What?" Defense and Disarmament News, February 1988.

Gold, Dore. "The INF Agreement: Implications for Europe and the Middle East." IDF Journal, Spring 1988.

Hirchfield, Thomas J. "Arms Control in Europe." Arms Control Today, March 1988.

Hosegewa, Tsuyoshi. Gorbachev's "New Thinking" in Soviet Foreign Security Policy and the Military--Recent Trends and Implications. Air War College Resident Studies NS 622, 1988.

Huge, De Santis. "After INF: The Political-Military Landscape of Europe." The Washington Quarterly, Summer 1988.

"Military Balance 1988/89." The International Institute for Strategic Studies, London, 1988.

"NATO and Warsaw Pact Force Comparisons." NATO Information Service, Brussels, 1984.

NATO Handbook. NATO Information Service, Brussels, April 1986.

"Negotiating the INF Treaty." Department of State Bulletin, March 1988.

Record, Jeffrey. "Defending Post-INF Europe." <u>Foreign Affairs</u>,
     Spring 1988.

Shanker, Thom. "Allies Answers Soviet Cuts." <u>Chicago Tribune</u>,
     22 December 1988.

Snyder, Jed C. "European Security After the INF Treaty, World
     and I." August 1988.

<u>Turkey Yearbook</u>, 1983. Prime Ministry Directorate General of
     Press and Information, Ankara, 1983.

"US Nuclear Weapon Programme." Air War College <u>Resident Studies
     DS 613</u>, 1988.